Darksi[de]

Teaching and Assessment Pack

www.heinemann.co.uk

✓ Free online support
✓ Useful weblinks
✓ 24 hour online ordering

01865 888118

Heinemann

Heinemann is an imprint of Pearson Education Limited, a company incorporated in England and Wales, having its registered office at Edinburgh Gate, Harlow, Essex, CM20 2JE. Registered company number: 872828

www.heinemann.co.uk

Heinemann is a registered trademark of Pearson Education Limited

Text © Pearson Education Limited 2008

First published 2008

12 11 10 09
10 9 8 7 6 5 4 3 2

British Library Cataloguing in Publication Data is available from the British Library on request.

ISBN 978 0 435131 99 9

Copyright notice
All rights reserved. The material in this publication is copyright. Pupil sheets may be freely photocopied for classroom use in the purchasing institution. However, this material is copyright and under no circumstances may copies be offered for sale. If you wish to use the material in any way other than that specified you must apply in writing to the publishers.

Typeset by Phoenix Photosetting, Chatham, Kent
Illustrations on page 10 by Martin Chatterton
Original illustrations © Pearson Education Limited 2008
Printed in Great Britain by Ashford Colour Press Ltd, Gosport, Hampshire

Acknowledgements

The author and publisher would like to thank the following individuals and organisations for permission to reproduce photographs on the CD Rom:

Image 4 © Getty Images/Stone; Image 5 © Dynamics Graphics; Image 6 © Tim Gartside/Alamy; Image 7 © Haraz Ghanbari/AP/PA Photos; Image 8 © Getty Images/Robert Harding World Imagery

Darkside
Tom Becker

Activities by Lucy English

Introduction

These extensive resources, produced to accompany *Darkside*, provide everything you need to plan and deliver engaging lessons and assess pupil progress.

The full scheme of work includes a medium-term overview and 15 individual lesson plans with accompanying student and teacher resource sheets as well as suggestions for homework. Guidance is provided throughout the scheme on assessing pupil progress, and the lessons build towards a final assessment task designed to measure progress in the skills developed during the preceding lessons. The QCA Assessing Pupil Progress grids have been re-written in student-friendly language for this scheme in a document entitled 'Assessment Guidelines grids'.

On the CD-ROM, in addition to electronic files of the entire contents of this book, you will find several video clips of the author discussing writers' craft, and images for use as visual stimulus material. Both the images and the video clips are referenced in the individual lesson plans where they are most relevant.

These resources are designed to appeal to a range of learning styles, and incorporate tasks explicitly matched to the 2008 Framework Objectives and Assessment Focuses without restricting you to a particular year group. They can be used to supplement your own teaching plans or to provide extra support for specific teaching points.

Resources for *Darkside*:

- Synopsis 2
- Medium-term overview 3
- Lesson plans and accompanying activity sheets 8
- Assessment Guideline grids 74

Synopsis

Jonathan Starling has always been an outsider. Having never known his mother and with a father who is either busy with his studies or in mental anguish in hospital, Jonathan's resulting self-sufficiency inevitably made school irrelevant. He has learnt to become invisible; to be left alone.

Which makes it even stranger that a mysterious intruder should break into the house at night, leaving animalistic gouges in the door Jonathan was hiding behind.

And when a woman with compelling, sleep-inducing perfume befriends him in the British Library it takes all his powers of ingenuity to break free.

Finally, his father rouses from his hospital bed to tell Jonathan to find a man he's never heard of: Carnegie, in a place he never knew existed: Darkside.

This fast-paced novel brings together classic Gothic elements with realistic modern characters. Jonathan never asked to be a hero, but deals with near-death experiences with increasing panache as the life-threatening situations mount up.

Darkside is 'the other side of the coin'; the place where 'the Ripper's' family are the only ones with enough evil to keep control; the place where people flock to see animals, perhaps humans, tear each other to pieces; the place where evil lurks on every street corner. It's an imaginative, action-packed place where you can't even pause for breath before someone tries to do you harm. It's a great place to set a novel.

This text allows direct teaching of structure and language, aspects of reading students often find so hard, while also having plenty of scope to explore character and characterisation, genre and plot. The wide range of settings, characters and events in the text allow for plenty of varied activities, addressing word, sentence, reading, writing and speaking and listening objectives in the Framework for teaching English, and the KS3 Assessment Focuses for reading, writing, speaking and listening.

Darkside medium-term overview

		Assessment focuses	2008 Framework objectives	Resources	Homework
Week 1	**Lesson 1**	**Reading AF2**: understand, describe, select or retrieve information, events or ideas from texts and use quotation and reference to text.	**3.2 Speaking and Listening**: roles in group discussion **5.1 Reading**: active reading skills	Resource 1.1 CD-ROM images 1, 2, 3 CD-ROM author interview 1	Research Gothic Literature and make a poster to illustrate and explain what it is.
	Lesson 2	**Reading AF3**: deduce, infer or interpret information, events or ideas from texts.	**5.1 Reading**: active reading skills	Assessment Guidelines – Reading grid Resource 2.1 CD-ROM author interview 2	Unpick a phrase or sentence.
	Lesson 3	**Reading AF5**: explain and comment on writers' use of language, including grammatical and literary features at word and sentence level. **Writing AF1**: write imaginative, interesting and thoughtful texts.	**6.2 Reading**: linguistic, grammatical and literary features **10.2 Language**: language use	Resources 3.1, 3.2, 3.3, 3.4 CD-ROM images 4, 5, 6 Scissors	Study and complete the positive and negative vocabulary worksheet (Resource 3.4).

Darkside medium-term overview

		Assessment focuses	2008 Framework objectives	Resources	Homework
Week 2	Lesson 4	**Reading AF3**: deduce, infer or interpret information, events or ideas from texts. **Writing AF7**: select appropriate and effective vocabulary.	**3.1 Speaking and Listening**: discussion skills and strategies **7.1 Writing**: ideas, planning and drafting **8.3 Writing**: improving vocabulary	Sticky notes A3 or poster paper for thoughtmaps Assessment Guidelines grids Resources 4.1, 4.2, 4.3	Advice to an actor playing a character.
	Lesson 5	**Writing AF5**: vary sentences for clarity, purpose and effect. **Writing AF6**: write with technical accuracy of syntax and punctuation …	**8.5 Writing**: structure, organisation and presentation **9.1 Writing**: standard English	Assessment Guidelines – Writing grid Resources 4.1, 5.1, 5.2 CD-ROM images 7, 8	Track a news story in different media to analyse style and language.
	Lesson 6	**Reading AF4**: identify and comment on the structure and organisation of texts, including grammatical and presentational features at text level. **Reading AF5**: explain and comment on writers' use of language, including grammatical and literary features at word and sentence level.	**5.1 Reading**: active reading skills **6.3 Reading**: organisation, structure, layout and presentation **8.2 Writing**: varying sentences and punctuation	Resources 6.1, 6.2, 6.3 CD-ROM author interview 3	Write about their journey to school using the techniques studied.

Darkside

Darkside medium-term overview

	Assessment focuses	2008 Framework objectives	Resources	Homework
Week 3 Lesson 7	**Reading AF6:** identify and comment on writers' purposes and viewpoints, and the overall effect of the text on the reader. **Writing AF7:** select appropriate and effective vocabulary.	6.2 **Reading:** linguistic, grammatical and literary features 10.2 **Language:** language usea	Mini whiteboards Resources 7.1, 7.2, 7.3	Research persuasive speeches.
Lesson 8	**Writing:** all AFs.	7.2 **Writing:** conventions and forms of texts 8.1 **Writing:** viewpoint, voice and ideas 8.4 **Writing:** linguistics and literary techniques	Assessment Guidelines – Writing grid Resource 8.1	Write a persuasive leaflet.
Lesson 9	**Reading AF4:** identify and comment on the structure and organisation of texts, including grammatical and presentational features at text level. **Writing:** the key AFs each student needs on an individual basis.	6.3 **Reading:** organisation, structure, layout and presentation	Marked work from last lesson Assessment Guidelines – Writing grid Resources 3.3, 9.1 CD-ROM author interview 4	Draw and label the plot structure of a text of their choice.

5

© Pearson Education Ltd, 2008

Darkside medium-term overview

Week 4

	Assessment focuses	2008 Framework objectives	Resources	Homework
Lesson 10	**Writing AF4:** construct paragraphs and use cohesion within and between paragraphs. **Writing AF5:** vary sentences for clarity, purpose and effect.	**8.2 Writing:** varying sentences and punctuation **10.2 Language:** language use	Assessment Guidelines – Writing grids Resources 10.1, 10.2, 10.3, 10.4, 10.5, 10.6	Make a poster to explain how complex sentences starting with adverbial phrases work.
Lesson 11	**Writing AF3:** organise and present whole texts effectively. **Writing AF4:** construct paragraphs and use cohesion within and between paragraphs. **Writing AF5:** vary sentences for clarity, purpose and effect.	**8.2 Writing:** varying sentences and punctuation **8.5 Writing:** structure, organisation and presentation	Assessment Guidelines – Writing grids Resources 11.1, 11.2	Write comparative sentences about any two subjects.
Lesson 12	**Speaking and Listening:** all AFs.	**4.2 Speaking and Listening:** techniques, conventions and styles **6.2 Reading:** linguistic, grammatical and literary features	Speaking and Listening grids Resources 9.1, 12.1, 12.2, 12.3 CD-ROM author interview 5	Produce a 'Missing' poster for one of the boys.

Darkside medium-term overview

	Assessment focuses	2008 Framework objectives	Resources	Homework
Week 5 Lesson 13	**Writing AF2:** produce texts which are appropriate to task, reader and purpose. **Writing AF3:** organise and present whole texts effectively. **Writing AF4:** construct paragraphs and use cohesion within and between paragraphs. **Writing AF6:** write with technical accuracy of syntax and punctuation …	7.2 **Writing:** conventions and forms of texts 8.1 **Writing:** viewpoint, voice and ideas 8.5 **Writing:** structure, organisation and presentation	A selection of tourist information leaflets Assessment Guidelines – Writing grid Resources 13.1, 13.2	Word process/use a DTP program to create the leaflet/webpages advertising Darkside as a tourist destination.
Lesson 14	**Reading AF4:** identify and comment on the structure and organisation of texts, including grammatical and presentational features at text level. **Reading AF6:** identify and comment on writers' purposes and viewpoints, and the overall effect of the text on the reader.	3.2 **Speaking and Listening:** roles in group discussion 6.2 **Reading:** linguistic, grammatical and literary features	Assessment Guidelines grids Resources 14.1, 14.2	Look at the AFs and personal targets to ensure meeting them in next lesson's assessment piece.
Lesson 15	Assessment Guidelines grids	Assessment	Assessment Guidelines grids	Write the opening of the next book in the series.

Homework has been suggested for every lesson but is not essential for Lesson 1.

Darkside by Tom Becker		Lesson 1
Class:	**Date:**	**Period:**

Lesson coverage:	Prologue Students will: explore conventions of the Gothic genre; find quotations in the text.
As a result of this lesson:	**All students will be able to**: identify features of Gothic Literature and refer to some from the text. **Most students will be able to**: select and discuss quotations that hook the reader and create the atmosphere. **Some students will be able to**: find a range of quotations that hook the reader and create atmosphere and explain how they work.

Assessment focus Reading AF2: understand, describe, select or retrieve information, events or ideas from texts and use quotation and reference to text.	Framework objectives 3.2 Speaking and Listening: taking roles in group discussion. 5.1 Reading: developing and adapting active reading skills and strategies.

Resources	• Resource 1.1 (Collective memory game) • CD-ROM: image 1 (Haunted house), 2 (Lightning), 3 (Shadow) • CD-ROM: author interview clip 1 (The Gothic genre – Tom Becker talks about Gothic as a genre and why he's written such a dark novel)

Personal teaching notes:	

© Pearson Education Ltd, 2008

Darkside by Tom Becker			Lesson 1
Class:	Date:		Period:
Starter	Organise students in teams of between three and five. Each student is allowed to come to the front to see Resource 1.1 for 15 seconds. They then return to their team and have 30 seconds to draw what they can remember before the next team member comes to the front to look at the resource. When everyone has had one or two goes (depends on class) time is up and the winning team is the one with the most accurate reproduction. Give teams 2 minutes to discuss and decide their strategy (for example, divide paper into grid, have a leader, etc.).		
Introduction	Ask students to study the elements of the sheet they have reproduced. Display Resource 1.1 on either a whiteboard or OHT. Ask students to suggest what title could go into the middle of the sheet. Take suggestions and shape the discussion to extract the title 'Gothic'. Show CD-ROM images 1, 2 and 3 and discuss with students what it is that makes these images gothic.		
Development	Either in groups or as a class read the Prologue of *Darkside*. Ask students to note down any gothic features or phrases. **Extension:** Ask students to identify the impact these features or phrases have on the reader. Show CD-ROM author interview clip 1.		
Plenary	Encourage students to share their findings while you elicit ideas about how the features hook the reader. Look for ideas about suspense, cliffhangers and clues. If there is time you could lead a discussion about the collective memory game (Resource 1.1). What group strategies worked? How did students have to work as a team?		
Homework	Ask students to research Gothic Literature and make a poster to illustrate and explain what it is.		

Darkside

1.1 Collective memory game

Study the following images. When you return to your team you will have 30 seconds to draw what you can remember.

© Pearson Education Limited, 2008

Darkside by Tom Becker		Lesson 2
Class:	Date:	Period:

Lesson coverage:	Chapters 1 and 2 Students will: unpick a phrase; study Assessment Guidelines – Reading grids; find evidence in the text.
As a result of this lesson:	**All students will be able to**: understand the need for textual evidence and select a quotation that creates a specific effect. **Most students will be able to**: select and discuss quotations that are relevant and unpick them to show how they work. **Some students will be able to**: find a range of quotations across the chapters and analyse the writer's intentions and techniques.

Assessment focus **Reading** AF3: deduce, infer or interpret information, events or ideas from texts.	**Framework objective** 5.1 **Reading:** developing and adapting active reading skills and strategies.

Resources	• Assessment Guidelines – Reading grids • Resource 2.1 (Unpick the phrase) • CD-ROM: author interview clip 2 (Isolated protagonists – Tom Becker discusses why it is that so many central protagonists are isolated in their everyday lives. Why does this have to be? What does it add to the fiction? What does it add for the reader?)
Personal teaching notes:	

Darkside by Tom Becker			Lesson 2
Class:	Date:		Period:
Starter	Recap words and phrases picked out in Lesson 1 and the impact they have on the reader. Write one of these phrases on the board and unpick it for the class. Show students how to do this, using Resource 2.1. (The sentence referred to in the resource is taken from page 1 of *Darkside*.) Then ask them to select a phrase each and do the same.		
Introduction	Show the Assessment Guidelines – Reading grid. Ask students to scan to find each time 'providing evidence' or a 'quotation' is mentioned. You might like to give them highlighters to do this task. Ask why evidence is so important. Point out that the task they have just done (the Starter) was itself close analytical reading. The amount of detail they have provided will determine the level. Tell the class that through the study of *Darkside* they are going to work on reading skills to ensure they move up the levels for reading.		
Development	Ask students to read Chapter 1 of *Darkside* and look for evidence about Jonathan Starling. They need to pull out key words and phrases that show his state of mind. Then they should choose one word or phrase to work with and unpick. Share ideas about Jonathan around the class and work towards identifying the fact that he is isolated. Show CD-ROM author interview clip 2. If there is time, discuss how the author has created this isolation. Repeat this task for Chapter 2 and ask students to share ideas that show us something bad is about to happen to Jonathan. How do we know?		
Plenary	Pose the questions: Why does the writer want us to realise Jonathan is isolated? How is this done? Refer back to the Assessment Guidelines – Reading grid. Ask students to identify the level they have worked at for this lesson and write down one key thing they need to do to improve next lesson.		
Homework	Ask students to find a phrase or sentence in a text that creates an atmosphere of fun/excitement/adventure – anything opposite to the phrases or sentences found in the lesson. Ask them to write it down and 'unpick' it.		

© Pearson Education Ltd, 2008

Darkside

2.1 Unpick the phrase

Study this example of how to unpick a phrase to examine its impact on the reader.

A small platoon of teachers struggled to subdue their rowdy pupils.

- Use of 'pupils', not 'students' is interesting. Makes them sound younger, more in need of teachers?

- Quieten down. Oppress? Not total oppression, just slight. Notice the alliterated 's' – what effect does the 's' sound have? Why used?

- Connotations of fighting, war, military, armies. Group of soldiers. Suggests the teachers are fighting the students? Sense of struggle? Conflict?

- Fight? Effort? Resist? Finding it hard, failing? Last bits of energy?

- Out of control. Noisy. Difficult. Lack of care or respect. In people's way. Disturbing others.

© Pearson Education Ltd, 2008

Darkside by Tom Becker		Lesson 3
Class:	Date:	Period:

Lesson coverage:	Chapters 3 and 4 Students will: investigate the power of verbs; understand 'pathetic fallacy'; apply the PEAI (Point, Evidence, Analysis, Impact) rule.
As a result of this lesson:	**All students will be able to**: identify key verbs and explain how they create the atmosphere in a text. **Most students will be able to**: use pathetic fallacy to add meaning to their writing. **Some students will be able to**: analyse how pathetic fallacy works.

Assessment focuses **Reading** **AF5**: explain and comment on writers' use of language, including grammatical and literary features at word and sentence level. **Writing** **AF1**: write imaginative, interesting and thoughtful texts.	Framework objectives **6.2 Reading**: analysing how writers' use of linguistic, grammatical and literary features shapes and influences meaning. **10.2 Language**: commenting on language use.

Resources	• Resources 3.1 (Verb power), 3.2 (Highlighting the verbs), 3.3 (PEAI rule), 3.4 (Positive and negative vocabulary) • CD-ROM: images 4 (Bad storm), 5 (Blazing heat), 6 (Autumn leaves) • Scissors

Personal teaching notes:

© Pearson Education Ltd, 2008

Darkside by Tom Becker — Lesson 3

Class:	Date:	Period:

Starter	Tell students they are about to take part in a verb sort. They cut up the verbs in Resource 3.1 and sort them in order of power (from most powerful to least powerful). This may be done in small groups using photocopies of Resource 3.1 or as a whole class on an interactive whiteboard. Discuss ideas and findings, and move onto the importance of verbs as the power in writing.
Introduction	Explain that verbs are key to much of writing. Show Resource 3.2 and ask students to highlight or identify the key verbs. **Extension:** Students look more closely at these verbs, unpicking the sentences in which they appear.
Development	Lead a class discussion about verbs that create atmosphere. Introduce the technical term 'pathetic fallacy', where natural things are given human emotions – in this case the weather. Ask students to pick out instances from Chapters 3 and 4 of *Darkside* where this is the case and discuss why it is a popular technique. Show CD-ROM images 4, 5 and 6, which all relate to the weather. Ask students to identify the emotions that these images suggest. **Extension:** To continue with the work on 'pathetic fallacy', you could refer to other texts such as Charles Dickens' *A Christmas Carol*.
Plenary	Allocate different tasks according to students' ability/working preferences. **Task 1:** Analyse the use of pathetic fallacy in *Darkside*, explaining why it is used and the impact it has on the reader. Use the PEAI rule (see Resource 3.3). **Task 2:** Look back at Resource 3.2. Ask students to imagine that Matthew has reached safety. They should write this paragraph, using pathetic fallacy. For example, the weather might change as his situation changes. They should then write a paragraph to analyse and explain their own writing.
Homework	Ask students to study and complete the positive and negative vocabulary worksheet (Resource 3.4). **Extension:** To state the word class for their choices (for example, verb, adjective, etc.).

Darkside

3.1 Verb power

Cut around the dotted lines, then sort these verbs into order of power – from most powerful to least powerful.

harassed	trembled
scurried	flickered
exploded	rolled
dripped	crammed
arrived	crashed
marched	crept
paused	raced
floated	hammered

© Pearson Education Ltd, 2008

3.2　Highlight the verbs

Darkside

Highlight or identify the key verbs in this passage. Then unpick these verbs.

As Matthew scuttled down the street the clouds sulked behind him, brooding and dark. He resisted the desire to look over his shoulder, preferring instead to try to get to safety before the bullies caught up with him. His fear drove him on as the rain started to spit down angrily and the skies threatened even worse.

'Great,' he thought, 'about to be beaten up and soaked. What have I done to deserve this?'

3.3 PEAI rule

PEAI stands for Point, Evidence, Analysis and Impact. When writing about writing, you should use the following structure.

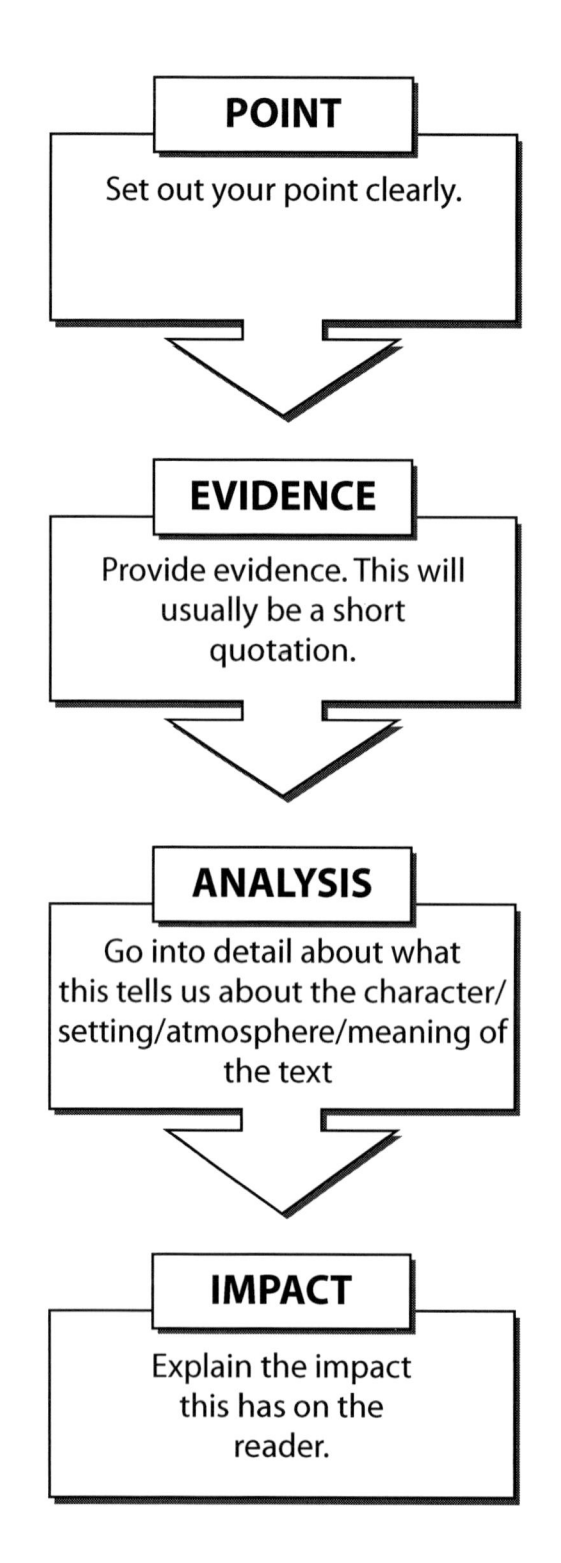

POINT
Set out your point clearly.

⬇

EVIDENCE
Provide evidence. This will usually be a short quotation.

⬇

ANALYSIS
Go into detail about what this tells us about the character/setting/atmosphere/meaning of the text

⬇

IMPACT
Explain the impact this has on the reader.

Darkside

3.4 Positive and negative vocabulary

1 Use a thesaurus and dictionary to find at least three positive and three negative words for each of the categories in the grid.

2 As an extension, you could jot down next to your chosen words the word class they come from (for example, verb, adjective, etc.).

	POSITIVE WORDS	NEGATIVE WORDS
A winter's day		
A supermarket		
A burger		

© Pearson Education Ltd, 2008

Darkside by Tom Becker — Lesson 4

Class:	Date:	Period:

Lesson coverage:	Chapters 1–7 Students will: explore character through inference; use modals; write a character profile.

As a result of this lesson:	**All students will be able to**: identify the main features of a character and structure these into a thoughtmap and written piece. **Most students will be able to**: use apt quotations to support their ideas. **Some students will be able to**: use modals to refine their analysis.

Assessment focuses **Reading** **AF3**: deduce, infer or interpret information, events or ideas from texts. **Writing** **AF7**: select appropriate and effective vocabulary.	**Framework objectives** **3.1 Speaking and Listening:** developing and adapting discussion skills and strategies in formal and informal contexts. **7.1 Writing:** generating ideas, planning and drafting. **8.3 Writing:** improving vocabulary for precision and impact.

Resources	• Sticky notes • A3 or poster paper for thoughtmaps • Assessment Guidelines – Writing grid • Resources 4.1 (Modal verbs), 4.2 (Character profile), 4.3 (Assessing character profile)

Personal teaching notes:

Darkside by Tom Becker — Lesson 4

Class:	Date:	Period:

Starter	Using enough sticky notes to go round the class, write the names: Jonathan, Dad, Mrs Elwood, Marianne, Humble, Skeet (one per sticky note). As students enter class, stick notes onto each student's forehead (differentiate – Humble and Skeet are harder). Students are not allowed to tell each other which character they are. They have to work it out for themselves by questioning other students. Explain that they can only ask closed questions (questions which are answered 'Yes' or 'No'). When students have established who they are, they should join others with the same name as them. Tell them they will continue to work in this 'name' group. Lead a discussion about the order of questions required. Establish that the 'big' ones were needed first – for example 'Am I male?'
Introduction	Ask students to quickly jot down all the questions they asked to identify who they were. This shows how much they already know about these characters. Explain that during this lesson they will investigate their character and use evidence, inference and deduction to write a profile of them. Students should arrange all their ideas into a thoughtmap, with different categories as different strands. Then they need to work through *Darkside* (including the Prologue) to add as much detail as possible to this thoughtmap. **Extension**: add evidence in the form of quotations.
Development	Use Resource 4.1 to recap modal verbs and discuss their use when using inference and deduction. Explain that students should try to use modals in their character profile. They should then write their profile either individually or as a group, depending on ability. Resource 4.2 may be used to scaffold this, as required.
Plenary	Distribute Resource 4.3 and instruct students to peer/self assess their written profiles. Students should compare the completed table to the Assessment Guidelines grids and note targets to focus on in the next lesson.
Homework	Ask students to imagine a film is being made of *Darkside*. The actor playing their character is struggling to understand the character. They should write a letter to the actor, explaining the key points that need to be borne in mind, and the aspects of the character that need to be emphasised. They could make up a back-story to explain the character. Explain that this letter will probably be less formal than their profile.

4.1 Modal verbs

1 Think about these modal verbs and discuss their use when using inference and deduction.

would

must

should

may

could

might

2 Now fit the correct verb into each sentence and explain why it works. (Remember: there could be more than one that makes sense. Try them to see how they change the meaning.)

a) Jane knew she _____ go to see her brother's concert, but she was really tired and didn't want to.

b) Although Kate _____ have another piece of chocolate, she decided to save it for later.

c) Although Sam knew the chocolate was Kate's and therefore _____ be left alone, he ate it anyway.

d) You _____ have my chocolate,' said Kate, sarcastically, when she found out.

e) I'd give it back, if I _____ ,' Sam replied, full of remorse.

f) Is there any chance you two _____ stop bickering?' asked Jane, who wondered if she _____ have gone to her brother's concert after all.

g) 'We _____ if we _____ ,' they replied and stomped out.

4.2 Character profile

Darkside

Use the PEAI rule to write about your character. You might like to use some of the following ideas and phrases in your profile.

- **The character's appearance**

  The nature of this character may be seen in his/her appearance ...
  Although this character looks ..., this appearance is deceptive ...

- **The character's actions**

  Actions such as ... suggest this character is ... .
  This character responds to events by ... . These actions might imply ...

- **The character's personality**

  This character is generally ... , suggesting ...
  What we know of this character's personality comes from actions such as ..., which suggest ...

- **The role this character will play in the story as a whole**

  This character is clearly the central protagonist and will play a key role. This is made clear by ...
  This character is minor but has an important function to perform ...

- **The reader's response to this character**

  We fear this character because ...
  We warm to this character because ...

- **Other ideas you could consider**
  - How this character interacts with other characters.
  - The function of this character in the chapters you've read.

Darkside

4.3 Assessing character profile (page 1 of 2)

Self or peer assess your character profiles. At what level have you met the Assessment Focuses?

Look at the statements and fill in the evidence to show what you have managed to do. You can check what level you have reached by comparing this with your Assessment Guidelines Reading and Writing grids.

Reading AF3: deduce, infer or interpret information, events or ideas from texts.

Have you done the following?	Evidence
Based your ideas on what you would think or feel.	
Made comments based on a single point in the text.	
Made comments based on different points in the text.	
Made comments that join the gaps between different points in the text.	
Made comments that join the gaps, and use evidence to support them.	
Made comments and suggested ideas that show different layers of meaning can exist at one time.	
Made comments that consider the wider implications of the ideas in the text.	
Made comments that pull together the ideas in the text and what the writer might be trying to make us think.	

Continued

4.3 Assessing character profile (page 2 of 2)

Darkside

> Writing AF7: select appropriate and effective vocabulary.

Have you used the following?	Evidence
Simple, generally appropriate vocabulary.	
Some deliberate vocabulary choices.	
Reasonably wide vocabulary used, though not always appropriately.	
Vocabulary chosen for effect.	
Vocabulary chosen for the audience and purpose.	
Ambitious vocabulary choices, even if they don't always work.	
Vocabulary well matched to audience and purpose.	
Varied and ambitious vocabulary choices that work well.	

Darkside by Tom Becker — Lesson 5

Class:	Date:	Period:

Lesson coverage:	Chapter 8 Students will: role-play; study Assessment Guidelines – Writing grid; write a formal report.
As a result of this lesson:	**All students will be able to**: understand how audience and purpose impacts language choice, and manipulate their language to fit this. **Most students will be able to**: exploit chronological connectives to add formality when appropriate for purpose and audience. **Some students will be able to**: analyse how meanings are changed when information is presented for different purposes and audiences.

Assessment focus **Writing** **AF5**: vary sentences for clarity, purpose and effect. **AF6**: write with technical accuracy of syntax and punctuation …	**Framework objectives** **8.5 Writing**: structuring, organising and presenting texts. **9.1 Writing**: using the conventions of standard English.

Resources	• Assessment Guidelines – Writing grid • Resources 4.1 (Modal verbs), 5.1 (Formal and informal vocabulary), 5.2 (Chronological connectives) • CD-ROM: images 7 (Police interview room), 8 (Trafalgar Square)

Personal teaching notes:

© Pearson Education Ltd, 2008

Darkside by Tom Becker		Lesson 5
Class:	Date:	Period:

Starter	Project CD-ROM image 7 or 8 as a background. Allocate roles according to ability (some characters are only briefly mentioned in the text): (from Prologue) Ricky's mum, Mr Watkins, tourists, Ricky's classmates; (from Chapters 1–7) Jonathan's teacher, Jonathan's classmates, Mrs Elwood, librarian; and police officers. Ask students to work in role and improvise the conversation between the police investigating the disappearance of Ricky and Jonathan and the possible witness or person who knows them. The police officers may take notes and the witness may use the novel, if desired.
Introduction	Pull together some of the ideas found and discuss the phrases that were heard often (probably phrases such as 'I don't really know' and 'He didn't really mix'). When such disappearances happen the police have to make formal reports which include both facts and supposition (although they need to make it clear when they are reporting supposition). Tell students they are going to write their version of the police report. Elicit the idea of modals being useful here. Use Resource 4.1 to recap modals if necessary. The language should also be formal. Discuss the possible structure (looking for a chronological structure) and connectives that might be used (*first, next, then, after that, finally*, etc.). As a class read Chapter 8.
Development	Distribute the Assessment Guidelines – Writing grid. Highlight the level students are working towards in AF5 and AF6. Students are to write the formal police report of the disappearance of either Ricky or Jonathan or both (depending on ability). Resources 5.1 and 5.2 may be used to support formal vocabulary choice and the use of chronological connectives.
Plenary	Begin a class discussion: Why does language and structure have to change according to purpose and audience? Why can't the police just report in our language? What difference does formality make?
Homework	Ask students to track one news story in different media – for example, national TV news, local TV news, national radio news, local radio news, Internet, national and local newspapers. How does the style and language change to match the audience?

Darkside

5.1 Formal and informal vocabulary

Complete 1–4 below providing alternative words and phrases according to audience and purpose.

> **Informal language: Tom talking to his mates**
> 'Yeah, Freddy lobbed the ball at me and it smashed the window, it was crazy, glass everywhere, Old Cooper going bonkers. I scarpered, quick.'

> **Formal language: Tom telling the same story to the head teacher**
> 'Well, sir. The ball came racing over towards me and, although I tried to stop it, I wasn't strong enough and it went through the window. I was scared and left the scene in order to find a teacher.'

1 Policeman talking to a judge in court:
   'I proceeded along the road.'

   Policeman talking to his colleagues on a tea break:
   '_____.'

2 Chef talking to his son:
   'Just bung all the stuff in a bowl and mix it together.'

   Chef describing the same process on a TV show:
   '_____.'

3 Hotel worker talking to a workmate, with no customers in earshot:
   'Grab some clean towels and chuck 'em here, will ya?'

   Hotel worker talking to the same workmate, with a customer standing nearby:
   '_____.'

4 The Queen talking to official visitors:
   '_____.'

   The Queen talking to her family in front of the TV:
   '_____.'

28

© Pearson Education Ltd, 2008

5.2 Chronological connectives

The connectives below can be used to help structure your report. If you use one at the beginning of each paragraph, your reader will see the events are moving on.

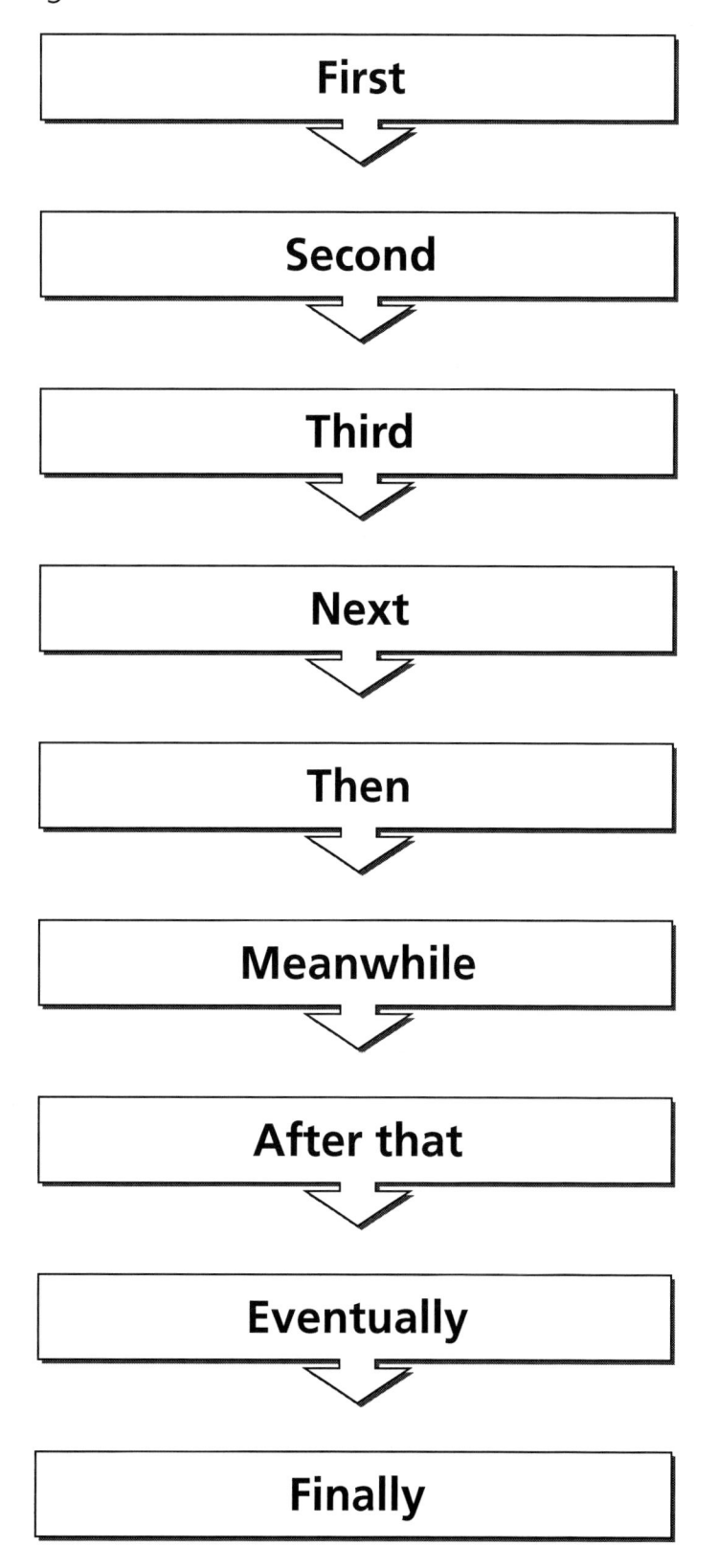

- First
- Second
- Third
- Next
- Then
- Meanwhile
- After that
- Eventually
- Finally

Darkside by Tom Becker			Lesson 6
Class:	Date:	Period:	

Lesson coverage:	Chapters 9–11 Students will: analyse the use of colons and semi-colons; explore plot structure.
As a result of this lesson:	**All students will be able to**: explain why colons are used and use a thoughtmap to make notes as they read. **Most students will be able to**: use semi-colons and explain the impact they have. **Some students will be able to**: analyse why an author uses complex punctuation and how it adds to the meaning of the text.

Assessment focuses Reading **AF4**: identify and comment on the structure and organisation of texts, including grammatical and presentational features at text level. **AF5**: explain and comment on writers' use of language, including grammatical and literary features at word and sentence level.	Framework objectives **5.1 Reading**: developing and adapting active reading skills and strategies. **6.3 Reading**: analysing writers' use of organisation, structure, layout and presentation. **8.2 Writing**: varying sentences and punctuation for clarity and effect.

Resources	• Resources 6.1 (Spot the difference), 6.2 (The semi-colon), 6.3 (Thoughtmap) • CD-ROM: author interview clip 3 (So much action – Tom Becker discusses why he packed in so much action; the sort of book he wanted to create and how he went about doing this)

Personal teaching notes:

© Pearson Education Ltd, 2008

Darkside by Tom Becker		Lesson 6
Class:	Date:	Period:

Starter	Show Resource 6.1 and ask students to discuss the difference between the sentences. The first sentence comes from page 70 of *Darkside*. They will notice the colon. Ask them to scan Chapter 9 to find a sentence that uses the colon in a similar way. (They will find another one on page 70.) From this they should make a rule about the use of the colon. Hear and refine their ideas until the class has a rule for the use of the colon that everyone is happy with.
Introduction	Show Resource 6.2 with the sentence from page 71 and look at the semi-colon. Ask students if they know why it has been used and what impact it has. Look at the fact that it is used to separate the main parts of the sentence and that commas are then used for the list of ideas described. If using on an interactive whiteboard, you can move the parts of the sentence to show the different elements it contains.

Mini-plenary: Discuss these questions: Why has so much been put in one sentence? Why not just write separate sentences? |
| Development | Students work in groups to recap Chapters 9, 10 and 11. Distribute copies of Resource 6.3. Give each student responsibility for a chapter or a section of a chapter and ask them to complete their thoughtmap as they read. Then ask groups to share their ideas, and discuss the plot and the way it has been structured. |
| Plenary | The events in *Darkside* are fast and furious. Discuss the following.
- What techniques has Tom Becker used to achieve this?
- Why might he want to create this impression?

Show CD-ROM author interview clip 3 regarding the questions above, and ask: What are you expecting from the book now? |
| Homework | Ask students to write about their journey to school. Remind them to think about the techniques Tom Becker has used and make their journey seem really exciting. (Tell them they may fictionalise it!) |

Darkside

6.1 Spot the difference

Read these sentences. How are they different? How does this change their impact?

> He had come out on to a narrow cobbled street that bubbled with a cauldron of voices: garbled shouts, throaty cries, squawks of protest and snarled threats.

> He had come out on to a narrow cobbled street that bubbled with a cauldron of voices and he heard garbled shouts, throaty cries, squawks of protest and snarled threats.

© Pearson Education Ltd, 2008

6.2 The semi-colon

Look at this sentence from page 71 of *Darkside*. Study the use of the semi-colon.

- Why do you think it has been used?
- What impact do you think it has?

> Every now and then he caught a fleeting glimpse of something that unnerved him: a gentleman with red lipstick smeared over his mouth grinned at his companion, revealing a set of sharp, protruding front teeth; a woman with the vacant eyes of a sleepwalker wandered past, nails clawing at her exposed skin; from somewhere in the folds of a dress or the confines of a suit, a blade glinted evilly.

Darkside

6.3 Thoughtmap

You will have been assigned a chapter, or a section of a chapter, by your teacher. Now complete this thoughtmap for those pages.

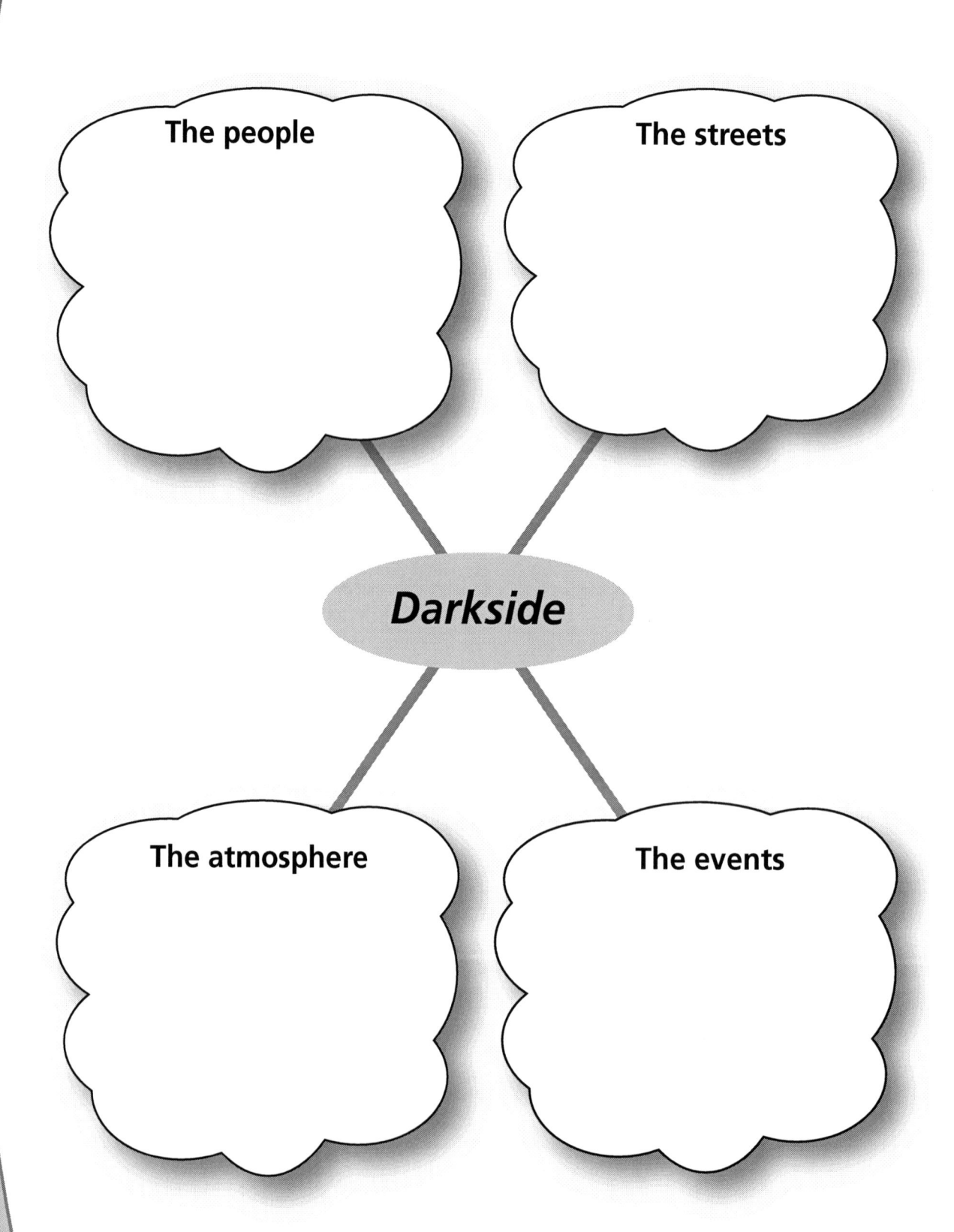

- **The people**
- **The streets**

Darkside

- **The atmosphere**
- **The events**

© Pearson Education Ltd, 2008

Darkside by Tom Becker			Lesson 7
Class:	**Date:**	**Period:**	

Lesson coverage:	Chapter 12 Students will: use emotive language; explore persuasive writing techniques; study an example of persuasive speech.
As a result of this lesson:	**All students will be able to**: identify the main purpose of a text. **Most students will be able to**: identify and explain the viewpoint of the writer. **Some students will be able to**: identify and explain the intended impact on the reader.

Assessment focuses Reading **AF6:** identify and comment on writers' purposes and viewpoints, and the overall effect of the text on the reader. Writing: **AF7:** select appropriate and effective vocabulary.	**Framework objectives** **6.2 Reading**: analysing how writers' use of linguistic, grammatical and literary features shapes and influences meaning. **10.2 Language**: commenting on language use.
Resources	• Mini whiteboards • Resources 7.1 (Emotive language), 7.2 (Getting your point across), 7.3 (Getting your point across – guided reading)

Personal teaching notes:

Darkside by Tom Becker — Lesson 7

Class:	Date:	Period:

Starter	Explain to students that the activity they are about to do will introduce them to emotive language. Distribute mini whiteboards and divide the class into two groups: Group A (who will write negative adjectives to describe the items you suggest) and Group B (who will write positive adjectives about the items). Call out items such as 'water', 'theme park' and 'dog'. Ask students to write at least three adjectives (positive or negative, according to their group) in the time available. Use Resource 7.1 for more ideas. Give 60 seconds for each category, then share ideas, relishing some of the adjectives they find – some might be onomatopoeic, which can be discussed. Discuss the power and importance of emotive language, and its role in involving the reader.
Introduction	Recap Chapter 12 and note down the details of Ricky's situation.
Development	Ask students to imagine they are Ricky. They have a chance to plead for freedom but to do this they will need better persuasive skills than Ricky – his words are useless. Show Resource 7.2 and ask students to read the text out loud to each other in groups. Use Resource 7.3 to guide students through the persuasive techniques used. If time, ask students to write down three emotive adjectives to describe the situation Ricky is in, then put them into a sentence.
Plenary	The rhetorical question 'And ain't I a woman?' was key to Sojourner Truth's speech (see Resources 7.2 and 7.3). Ask students to devise, write down and share a rhetorical question Ricky could use in his speech, pleading for freedom. Which persuasive techniques would they use and why?
Homework	Ask students to research other persuasive speeches and write down examples of emotive language, pattern of three, repetition, rhetorical questions and exclamations used. For examples, suggest they look online at the speeches made by Robin Cook and Tony Blair on 18 March 2003 and the 'I have a dream speech' by Martin Luther King.

Darkside

7.1 Emotive language

Write down as many adjectives as you can for each category. Some suggestions have been made to get you thinking.

	Positive	Negative
School dinners	nutritious filling mouthwatering	mouldy rancid putrid
A tabloid paper		
A TV Show		
A machine		
Skiing		
Rain		
A teddy bear		
A pizza		

© Pearson Education Ltd, 2008

7.2 Getting your point across

In groups, read this text out loud to each other. It comes from a speech by Sojourner Truth (a women's rights activist) and was delivered in 1851 to the Women's Convention in Akron, Ohio.

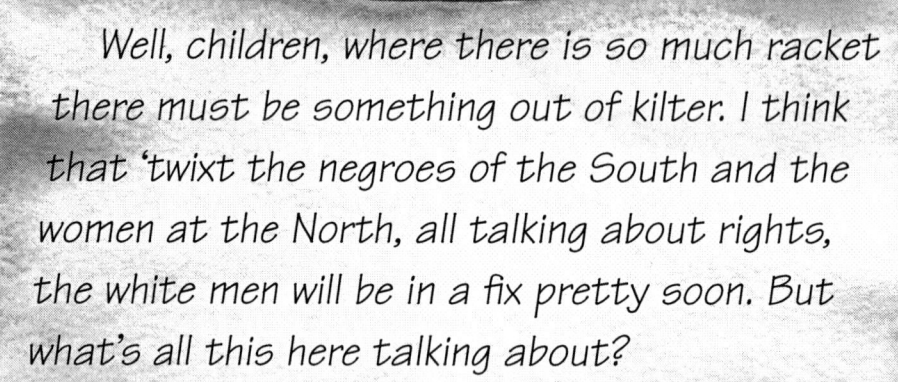

> Well, children, where there is so much racket there must be something out of kilter. I think that 'twixt the negroes of the South and the women at the North, all talking about rights, the white men will be in a fix pretty soon. But what's all this here talking about?
>
> That man over there says that women need to be helped into carriages, and lifted over ditches, and to have the best place everywhere. Nobody ever helps me into carriages, or over mud-puddles, or gives me any best place! And ain't I a woman? Look at me! Look at my arm! I have ploughed and planted, and gathered into barns, and no man could head me! And ain't I a woman? I could work as much and eat as much as a man - when I could get it - and bear the lash as well! And ain't I a woman? I have borne thirteen children, and seen most all sold off to slavery, and when I cried out with my mother's grief, none but Jesus heard me! And ain't I a woman?

From *Ain't I a Woman*, a speech by Sojourner Truth

Darkside

7.3 Getting your point across – guided reading

Look again at Sojourner Truth's speech 'Ain't I a woman?'. This time, think about the persuasive techniques she has used to make her listeners think.

> Well, children, where there is so much racket there must be something out of kilter. I think that 'twixt the negroes of the South and the women at the North, all talking about rights, the white men will be in a fix pretty soon. But what's all this here talking about?
>
> That man over there says that women need to be helped into carriages, and lifted over ditches, and to have the best place everywhere. Nobody ever helps me into carriages, or over mud-puddles, or gives me any best place! And ain't I a woman? Look at me! Look at my arm! I have ploughed and planted, and gathered into barns, and no man could head me! And ain't I a woman? I could work as much and eat as much as a man – when I could get it – and bear the lash as well! And ain't I a woman? I have borne thirteen children, and seen most all sold off to slavery, and when I cried out with my mother's grief, none but Jesus heard me! And ain't I a woman?

Annotations:

- **Rhetorical question to engage the audience** (pointing to "But what's all this here talking about?")
- **Creates sense of self and other – distances and rejects him** (pointing to "That man over there")
- **List of three: helped, lifted, have... best**
- **Demands attention: passionate and dramatic – does she show her arm? What impact does this physical gesture have?** (pointing to "Look at me! Look at my arm!")
- **Uses same list of three herself!** (helps, over, gives)
- **And another list of three!** (ploughed, planted, gathered)
- **Another list of three** (work, eat, bear)
- **What about this repeated rhetorical question? Why is it used all the time? What impact does it have?** (And ain't I a woman?)
- **Guess what? Another list of three – what is the point of working in threes? What does it do?** (borne, seen, cried)

39

© Pearson Education Ltd, 2008

Darkside by Tom Becker		Lesson 8
Class:	Date:	Period:

Lesson coverage:	Students will: study the Assessment Guidelines – Writing grid; write a persuasive speech.
As a result of this lesson:	**All students will be able to**: use at least one persuasive technique to write a persuasive speech. **Most students will be able to**: use more than one technique. **Some students will be able to**: craft their speech to manipulate the audience.

Assessment focus **Writing**: all AFs.	Framework objectives **7.2 Writing**: using and adapting the conventions and forms of texts. **8.1 Writing**: developing viewpoint, voice and ideas. **8.4 Writing**: developing varied linguistics and literary techniques.

Resources	• Assessment Guidelines – Writing grid • Resource 8.1 (Keeping the audience onside)
Personal teaching notes:	

Darkside by Tom Becker — Lesson 8

Class:	Date:	Period:

Starter	Show students Resource 8.1 and ask them to discuss what persuasive techniques are being used. Pull together the idea of collective pronouns as a powerful way to persuade and list these on the board.
Introduction	Recap the persuasive rhetorical questions students wrote at the end of Lesson 7 and the impact they are meant to have. Explain that students will now use the persuasive techniques they have learnt to write a persuasive speech that will be assessed for writing. Show the Assessment Guidelines – Writing grid and recap the AFs. Ask students how a persuasive speech might address each AF. (You can give different AFs to different groups.)
Development	Students write their persuasive speeches.
Plenary	Encourage students to give an initial peer assessment of their speeches, using the Assessment Guidelines – Writing grid. If necessary, model this first. You may wish to collect these pieces of work and mark them yourself, also using the Assessment Guidelines – Writing grid.
Homework	Ask students to write a leaflet to persuade *Darkside* inhabitants to visit the fight.

8.1 Keeping the audience onside

Think about the psychology of persuasion. What persuasive techniques are being used here?

> We all know the Internet is fun, but have we really thought about its potential for bullying?

> So what can we do? How can we protect our park from the money-hungry developers? It's up to us and we can make a difference …

> Join us today, and together we can change the world!

Darkside by Tom Becker			Lesson 9
Class:	Date:		Period:

Lesson coverage:	Chapters 13 and 14 Students will: explore plot structure; understand the key terms 'protagonist' and 'antagonist'; undertake a character analysis of Vendetta.
As a result of this lesson:	**All students will be able to**: map the plot of a text and understand the role of the central protagonist and antagonist. **Most students will be able to**: consider why a text is structured in certain ways and use this to make predictions. **Some students will be able to**: apply the concept of equilibrium when analysing the plot structure of a text of their choosing.

Assessment focuses Reading **AF4**: identify and comment on the structure and organisation of texts, including grammatical and presentational features at text level. Writing: the key **AF**s each student needs on an individual basis	Framework objectives **6.3 Reading**: analysing writers' use of organisation, structure, layout and presentation.

Resources	• Marked persuasive speeches from last lesson • Assessment Guidelines – Writing grid • Resources 3.3 (PEAI rule), 9.1 (Plot graph) • CD-ROM: author interview clip 4 (Vendetta! – Tom Becker discusses the character Vendetta, and why he is introduced late in the story)

Personal teaching notes:

Darkside by Tom Becker — Lesson 9

Class:	Date:	Period:

Starter	Return speeches with assessments made on Assessment Guidelines – Writing grid. Put students in groups of similar ability to discuss their work and look at what they need to do to move up a level. If appropriate, some students could read out their speeches.
Introduction	Display Resource 9.1 and ask students to work out which labels should go where. If possible, have this on a whiteboard to drag and drop the labels. Explain the key terms and the fact that some novels have many reversals and rising actions. Explain the terms 'protagonist' and 'antagonist', highlighting the prefixes that help us to understand these two terms.
Development	A new character, Vendetta, is introduced in Chapters 13 and 14. Ask students for their initial impressions of him but refuse to accept any until they provide evidence. Students should use the PEAI rule to write an analysis of at least one *Darkside* character – according to ability (review Resource 3.3). Remind them to look at the Assessment Guidelines – target they set earlier in the lesson.
Plenary	Discuss why Vendetta has been introduced at this stage. Show CD-ROM author interview clip 4 to check whether correct. **Extension:** introduce the idea of equilibrium. Students can then complete the definitions on Resource 9.1.
Homework	Ask students to draw and label the plot structure of another text of their choice. This could be anything from a children's story to a film or an episode of a TV soap opera. They should try to predict what it will look like before they start!

© Pearson Education Ltd, 2008

Darkside

9.1 Plot graph

This is the basic shape of a novel. Fill in the labels and try to identify a part of *Darkside* to match each one.

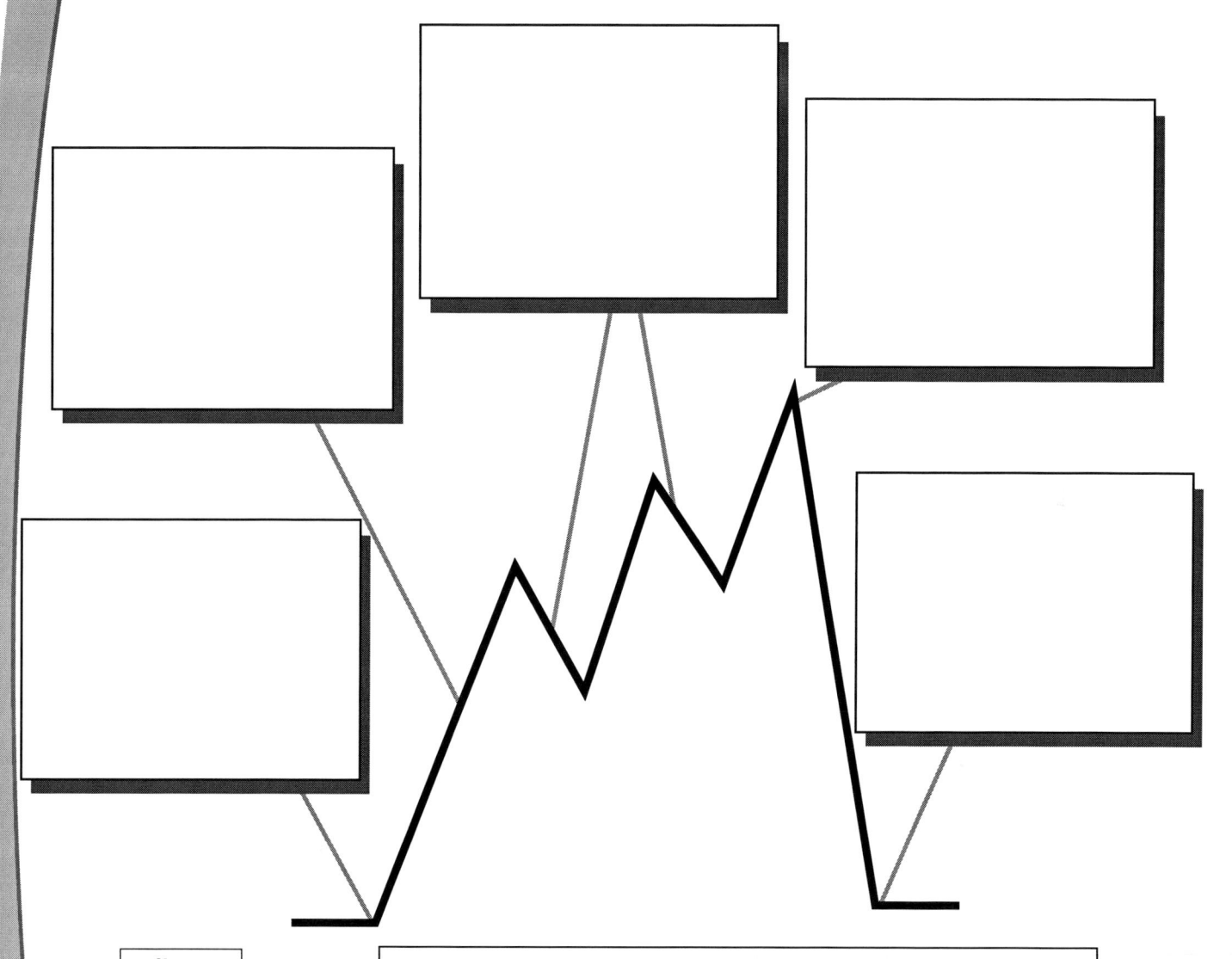

| climax |
| reversal |
| precipitating action |
| resolution |
| rising action |

- **Climax:** the most exciting part where the outcome is decided
- **Reversal:** something or someone prevents the main protagonist from following their path to achieve their goal
- **Precipitating action:** the event that starts the plot rolling
- **Resolution:** all is right again and equilibrium is restored
- **Rising action:** events building up

Extension: Complete the definitions.

Protagonist: _____

Antagonist: _____

Equilibrium: _____

© Pearson Education Ltd, 2008

Darkside by Tom Becker			Lesson 10
Class:	Date:		Period:

Lesson coverage:	Chapter 15 Students will: use adverbial phrases; explore the effect of a variety of sentence types.
As a result of this lesson:	**All students will be able to**: arrange adverbial clauses to create sentences with impact. **Most students will be able to**: write their own adverbial clauses to craft their writing. **Some students will be able to**: use a variety of sentence structures to craft their descriptive writing.

Assessment focuses Writing **AF4**: construct paragraphs and use cohesion within and between paragraphs. **AF5**: vary sentences for clarity, purpose and effect.	Framework objectives **8.2 Writing**: varying sentences and punctuation for clarity and effect. **10.2 Language**: commenting on language use.
Resources	• Assessment Guidelines – Writing grid • Resources 10.1 (Sentence types), 10.2 (Unpick the sentence), 10.3 (Unpick the sentence teacher resource), 10.4 (Sentence structure), 10.5 (Crafting your writing), 10.6 (How's my writing?)

Personal teaching notes:

Darkside by Tom Becker — Lesson 10

Class:	Date:	Period:

Starter	Use Resource 10.1 to recap and consolidate with students understanding of simple, compound and complex sentences. Discuss the definitions students come up with and write whole-class definitions on the board or a poster for all to see during the lesson.
Introduction	Read Chapter 15 and ask students to make notes on the question: How do we know there is something wrong with the police investigation? Take comments, with evidence, and discuss the students' ideas.
Development	Show Resource 10.2 and ask the students to unpick the sentence. Support for this is on Resource 10.3. Either use Resource 10.4 or an interactive whiteboard to move the parts of the sentence around to show how it can be written differently but still mean the same. Lead a discussion about the impact of the complex sentences, especially when followed by the very short simple sentences.

Use Resource 10.5 as an exercise to structure students' own writing. You may like to lead them through these ideas. |
| **Plenary** | Use Resource 10.7 to support self/peer assessment. Use Assessment Guidelines – Writing grid to identify levels and set individual writing targets. |
| **Homework** | Ask students to write a paragraph describing a character, like Jonathan, who is trying to stay hidden. Ask them to use some adverbial phrases and at least one simple, one compound and one complex sentence. |

Darkside

10.1 Sentence types

Look at the examples of simple, compound and complex sentences. Write a definition of each sentence type.

Simple sentences
- Sam is incredibly excited.
- The old ghost was very tired.
- My very hairy silver cat always tries to sleep on my black wool coat.

Now define it
A simple sentence is:
_____
_____

Compound sentences
- Sam walked to the shop and bought a magazine.
- The old ghost was very tired but still tried to scare Wayne.
- I always have to clean cat hair off my black wool coat and it makes me cross.

Now define it
A compound sentence is:
_____
_____

Complex sentences
- Sam, who is incredibly excited, is going to Australia for a holiday.
- Although tired, the old ghost still tried to scare Wayne.
- The old ghost, who was very tired, tried to scare Wayne.
- My very hairy silver cat always tries to sleep on my black wool coat; I have to spend hours cleaning cat hair off it.

Now define it
A complex sentence is:
_____
_____

© Pearson Education Ltd, 2008

10.2 Unpick the sentence

Read this extract from Chapter 15, page 112 of *Darkside*, then unpick it.

> Glancing furtively up and down the street, he checked to make sure that no one was watching him. It was empty.

Darkside

10.3 Unpick the sentence (teacher resource)

Use these questions and prompts to guide the students in unpicking this extract.

What sort of phrase has been used to start this sentence?

What does 'furtively' mean? What does it sound like? How long does it take to say? What does it suggest, especially when put with 'glancing'?

What impact does the pronoun have?

Glancing furtively up and down the street, he checked to make sure that no one was watching him. It was empty.

What has been used at the end here? Why has a very short simple sentence been used after the complex sentence? What impact does it have? What is the writer trying to do?

What does this suggest? Why is it at the end of the sentence? What impact does that have?

© Pearson Education Ltd, 2008

Darkside

10.4 Sentence structures

Read this sentence.

Glancing furtively up and down the street, he checked to make sure that no one was watching him. It was empty.

Look at these examples of how it can be written differently but still mean the same.

> He checked, glancing furtively up and down the street, to make sure that no one was watching him. It was empty.

> He checked to make sure that no one was watching him by glancing furtively up and down the street. It was empty.

> Checking to make sure that no one was watching, he glanced furtively up and down the street. It was empty.

© Pearson Education Ltd, 2008

Darkside

10.5 Crafting your writing

We've done a lot of work on language and vocabulary, now we need to look at the way in which sentences are structured. All sentence types are useful – remember the impact of that short simple sentence 'It was empty' (*Darkside*, page 112) – but the wider the range you have, the more power you can give your writing. In this task you will learn to use adverbial phrases to control the pace and impact of your writing.

1 Look at this sentence:

   Down the path, at the end of the garden, under the tree, the treasure glinted.

   a) Highlight the three words in this sentence that tell you what is really happening.

   b) By using three adverbial phrases to lead up to this clause the writer takes us to the treasure. Why is it effective?

2 Now imagine the treasure is glinting away elsewhere, maybe indoors? Maybe in your shoe? Write three different adverbial phrases to lead us to the treasure.

   _____ , _____ ,

   _____ , the treasure glinted.

   Obviously, you don't just have to use treasure, but this type of sentence leads the reader to the end point, so it's got to be something important. Look at what happens when this sentence is followed with a very short simple sentence:

   Down the path, at the end of the garden, under the tree, the treasure glinted. Nathan grinned.

3 Write a short description of one of the following ideas. Use adverbial phrases to start your first sentence. Think about the length any following sentences might be – be prepared to play around to make the maximum impact. This activity is about crafting really good writing, not about the amount you can write.

   - An empty shopping centre at night
   - A haunted house
   - The sea
   - A loud and chaotic classroom
   - A messy bedroom

Darkside

10.6 How's my writing? (page 1 of 2)

Write down the evidence next to the statements that most match your writing. You can check what level you are working at by looking at your Assessment Guidelines – Writing grid.

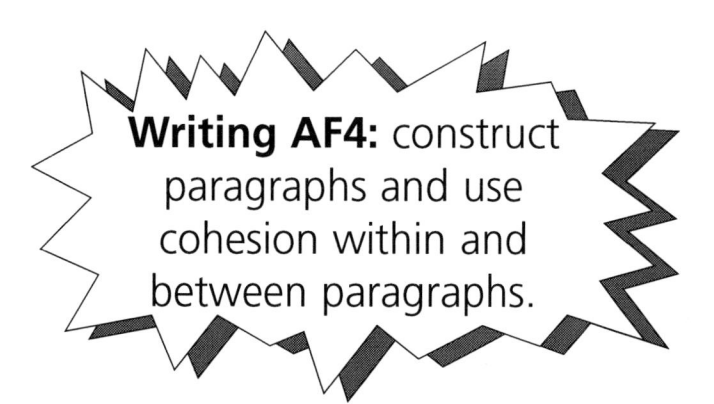

Writing AF4: construct paragraphs and use cohesion within and between paragraphs.

Have you done the following?	Evidence
Write paragraphs that are one or more sentences long.	
Used paragraphs to help organise the content.	
Used some connectives.	
Been consistent in your use of chronological connectives.	
Used connectives and pronouns to make your ideas flow and easy to follow.	
Used connectives, pronouns and adverbials to add emphasis to your ideas.	
Shaped each paragraph so your writing is balanced and your ideas flow.	
Used paragraphs to add meaning and purpose to your writing and manipulate the reader's response.	

Continued

10.6 How's my writing? (page 2 of 2)

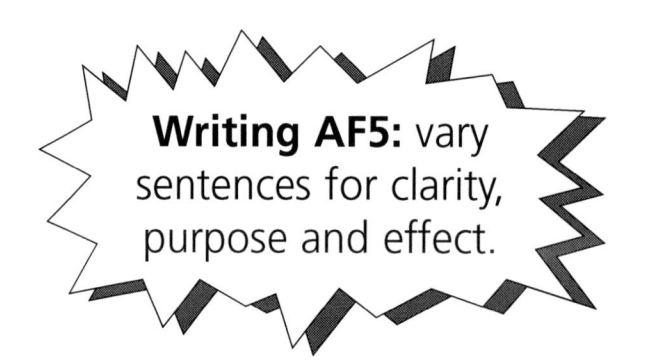

Darkside

Writing AF5: vary sentences for clarity, purpose and effect.

Have you used the following?	Evidence
Used simple sentences and 'and' and 'but' to connect ideas.	
Some variation in sentence lengths and types.	
Variation in word order to create specific effects.	
A variety of sentence lengths and types to create emphasis.	
Controlled use of a variety of simple, compound and complex sentences to achieve specific effects.	
Specific sentence features such as adverbial phrases to start sentences in order to create specific effect.	
Shaped and crafted sentences that allow the writing to flow.	
Carefully considered sentence lengths and structures for specific purpose and effect.	

Darkside by Tom Becker — Lesson 11

Class:	Date:	Period:

Lesson coverage:	Chapters 16–19 Students will: explore the nature and uses of connectives; further explore plot structure and characterisation.

As a result of this lesson:	**All students will be able to**: compare using connectives. **Most students will be able to**: use those connectives for cohesion. **Some students will be able to**: consider character function in their analysis.

Assessment focuses Writing **AF3**: organise and present whole texts effectively … **AF4**: construct paragraphs and use cohesion within and between paragraphs. **AF5**: vary sentences for clarity, purpose and effect.	**Framework objectives** **8.2 Writing**: varying sentences and punctuation for clarity and effect. **8.5 Writing**: structuring, organising and presenting texts.

Resources	• Assessment Guidelines – Writing grid • Resources 11.1 (Connective categories), 11.2 (Comparing characters)

Personal teaching notes:

Darkside by Tom Becker — Lesson 11

Class:	Date:	Period:

Starter	Use Resource 11.1 to sort the connectives list into categories. Discuss with students what they are, what they do and when they are used. Ask students to look at the Assessment Guidelines – Writing grid and find which AFs will be met by using connectives. (Answer: **AF3, AF4** and **AF5**.)
Introduction	In Chapters 16–18 we find out more about the two boys, Ricky and Jonathan; and the Darkside characters, Carnegie and Marianne. Ask students to work in groups to compare one of these pairs. (Allocate according to ability.) Ask them to go back through the book and make notes about the characters they are focusing on, using Resource 11.2.
Development	Look at all the ideas the groups have amassed. The key to communicating these ideas in a clear and logical way is to use connectives. Look back at the connectives on Resource 11.1 and show students how these can be used to join ideas together in the middle of compound or complex sentences, but can also be used at the start of sentences and paragraphs to signal to the reader. Look back at the Assessment Guidelines – Writing grid for an explanation of what connectives can do if well used.

Select some of the ideas the students have found and demonstrate how to write them as a comparative analysis, using connectives. Students should then work individually or in pairs to write sentences about their characters, using connectives to structure the comparison. |
| **Plenary** | Share and comment on the effectiveness of the sentences. Ask students to use the Assessment Guidelines – Writing grid to assess how they have used connectives. |
| **Homework** | Ask students to write comparative sentences. They might like to choose from:
• two soap operas
• two bands
• two sports
• two brands of fizzy drink
• two types of food. |

Darkside

11.1 Connective categories

Sort the connectives at the bottom of this page into the following categories.

Starting off

Driving along

Moving on up

Doing a U-turn

Coming to a stop

Connectives

but	and	finally	to start with	although
however	in conclusion		moreover	second
first	third	also	therefore	alternatively
conversely	because	in addition		while

57

© Pearson Education Ltd, 2008

Darkside

11.2 Comparing characters

Make notes about your characters under the following headings. Remember to put page references so you can find evidence again.

	Character 1 _____	Character 2 _____
Appearance		
Skills/abilities		
Personality		
Status		
Relationships with others		
Plot function		
How does the reader respond? Why?		

Darkside by Tom Becker			Lesson 12
Class:	**Date:**	**Period:**	

Lesson coverage:	Chapter 19 Students will: consolidate the use of connectives; self-assess against the Speaking and Listening Assessment Focuses; role-play to present a TV show.
As a result of this lesson:	**All students will be able to**: evaluate their Speaking and Listening drama role-play. **Most students will be able to**: analyse the characters and clues laid down in the text. **Some students will be able to**: use talk to probe and manipulate others in role.

Assessment focuses **Speaking and Listening** All **AFs**.	**Framework objectives** **4.2 Speaking and Listening**: developing, adapting and responding to dramatic techniques, conventions and styles. **6.2 Reading**: analysing how writers' use of linguistic, grammatical and literary features shapes and influences meaning.
Resources	• Assessment Focuses Speaking and Listening grids • Resources 9.1 (Plot graph), 12.1 (Connectives bingo), 12.2 (StopCrimeUK), 12.3 (Evaluating Speaking and Listening) • CD-ROM: author interview clip 5 (Cliffhangers – Tom Becker talks about keeping the reader hooked)
Personal teaching notes:	

Darkside by Tom Becker		Lesson 12
Class:	Date:	Period:

Starter	Distribute Resource 12.1 and ask students to fill in one connective for each category. Weaker students may be given sheets with some already filled in.

If suggested homework for Lesson 11 was completed, students use these for the following activity. If not, ask students to quickly write a sentence, using a connective, that compares two TV programmes.

Ask students to read out one of their sentences. If the connective(s) they have used are on a bingo sheet, that student gets to cross them off. The winner is the person to cross off all their connectives first … except … you could have a class discussion about the fact the more unusual connectives are the ones that are left, and therefore might be ones to aim to use. |
| **Introduction** | As a class, read Chapter 19 and then recap the events in Chapter 18, especially the final sentence. Discuss how this sentence is effective as a cliffhanger or hook for the reader. Why do authors need to use these techniques? Show CD-ROM author interview clip 5 on cliffhangers.

Distribute Resource 9.1 and ask students to add details from the book to show the rising action and reversals. Ensure students mark on all the chapters that focus on the police investigation. Why are these sections interspersed throughout the book? |
Development	Put students into mixed-ability groups and use Resource 12.2 to prepare a performance of the new TV programme 'StopCrimeUK'. Distribute Resource 12.3.
Plenary	Watch performances and ask students to complete Resource 12.3.
Homework	Ask students to produce a 'Missing' poster for one of the boys.

Darkside

12.1 Connectives bingo

Write one connective that matches each category.

Starting off	Driving along
Moving on up	Doing a U-turn
Coming to a stop	

12.2 StopCrimeUK!

You have been asked to prepare a performance of the new TV programme *StopCrimeUK*. Use the information below to help you.

Memo

To: the director of this new, informative, public information programme

From: the TV Controller

Subject: Missing London schoolboys – Ricky Thomas and Jonathan Starling

---

Message

The public are really interested in this story – two schoolboys going missing and no apparent witnesses. I want you to cover the story in this week's edition of the programme.

Try to get a police witness, maybe PC Shaw as he's more media friendly, but if you can also get Carter Roberts that'll be interesting – just make sure he's handled carefully.

Let's go for the human interest angle on this one – maybe try to get some of their school friends and teachers? Any parents? Guardians? Just get as much information as you can!

I look forward to seeing the programme. Remember, we want to be known for being:

- clear and to the point – the structure must be easily followed so make sure you use connectives and verbal flags so the viewers can follow

- purposeful – make it clear why each presenter or witness is there and what they have to contribute

- easy to follow – this might be through non-verbal communication as well as verbal

- thorough – the whole piece has drive and sustains the focus.

Darkside

12.3 Evaluating Speaking and Listening

Look at the Assessment Focuses and comment on what you have achieved. Try to provide evidence for each achievement. Then, work out what you could do to improve.

Assessment Focuses	How did I do?	Evidence	Next time?
1 Talk in purposeful and imaginative ways to explore ideas and feelings, using non-verbal features for clarity and effect.			
2 Listen and respond to others, identifying main ideas, implicit meanings and viewpoints, and how these are presented.			
3 Adapt and vary structures and vocabulary according to purpose, listeners and what is spoken about, including selecting and using the features of spoken standard English effectively.			
4 Make a range of contributions when working in groups, shaping meanings through suggestions, comments and questions and drawing ideas together.			
5 Create and sustain different roles, adapting techniques in a range of dramatic activities to explore texts, ideas and issues.			

Darkside by Tom Becker		Lesson 13
Class:	Date:	Period:

Lesson coverage:	Chapters 20–24 Students will: write an information leaflet; use the Assessment Guidelines – Writing grid.
As a result of this lesson:	**All students will be able to**: write an information leaflet about Darkside using subheadings. **Most students will be able to**: use more than one technique. **Some students will be able to**: layout their ideas for maximum effect.

Assessment focuses **Writing** **AF2**: produce texts which are appropriate to task, reader and purpose. **AF3**: organise and present whole texts effectively … **AF4**: construct paragraphs and use cohesion within and between paragraphs. **AF6**: write with technical accuracy of syntax and punctuation …	**Framework objectives** **7.2 Writing**: using and adapting the conventions and forms of texts. **8.1 Writing**: developing viewpoint, voice and ideas. **8.5 Writing**: structuring, organising and presenting texts.

Resources	• A selection of tourist information leaflets (these can be collected in advance by students) • Assessment Guidelines – Writing grid • Resources 13.1 (Welcome to Citytown), 13.2 (Analysing information leaflets)

Personal teaching notes:

Darkside by Tom Becker		Lesson 13
Class:	Date:	Period:
Starter	As a class, look at Resource 13.1 and/or the selection of tourist information leaflets you/students have collected. Ask students to scan through and make notes about them on Resource 13.2. Draw together findings, emphasising how the language, structure and layout fits the purpose and audience. **Extension**: Analyse websites that provide similar information.	
Introduction	Ask students to gather information for a tourist information leaflet about Darkside. They need to go through the chapters that refer to Darkside and make notes.	
Development	Ask students to write a tourist information leaflet for Darkside. Remind them to use the techniques found in Resource 13.1 and the selection of tourist leaflets gathered for the Starter activity. Tell them not to worry about layout yet but to concentrate on the text. **Extension**: Write the text for a website.	
Plenary	Ask students to peer assess the text composed for the leaflet/website and use the Assessment Guidelines – Writing grid to see at what level the AFs are being met. Remind students they are doing a final written task in Lesson 15, so they need to know what they must do to improve their level.	
Homework	Ask students to word process/use a DTP program to create the leaflet/webpages they have made. Put in the text, then manipulate the layout for maximum impact and effect on the reader.	

13.1 Welcome to Citytown

Scan through the information below. Your teacher will ask you to make some notes about it on Resource 13.2.

Welcome to Citytown!

With our flowing river and charming streets full of friendly local shops, we have everything you might want. From family days out, playing games on the green, to a serious search in our shops for your dream item, all are catered for at Citytown.

The river

Follow the flow of the river on a peaceful stroll through beautiful countryside and enjoy our fabulous fresh air. Don't forget some bread for the ducks who are sure to come up to say hello!

The green

Unlike many towns, we see our green as an active part of the community so you won't see any 'Keep off the grass' signs! Instead, you are invited to play games, picnic and generally enjoy the beauty of the town.

The shops

We are privileged to have a wide selection of chain and independent shops, all carrying a fine selection of goods. You are sure to find all you could want here. Furthermore, with our fine crafts people, offering handmade jewellery, you can always commission a piece to your exact requirements.

The theatre

It may only be small, but our theatre is at the heart of the community and has a wide variety of productions. Join us and be amazed and entertained.

Recreation facilities

With youth club, tea shops, the theatre and a thriving football club we've got something for everyone.

What more could you want? Why not visit us today?

Transport

Buses run regularly from the train station at Upper City. We also have two well-maintained car parks for those who are driving in. Just follow the clear signs from the motorway.

13.2 Analysing information leaflets

Make notes below about the information on Resource 13.1.

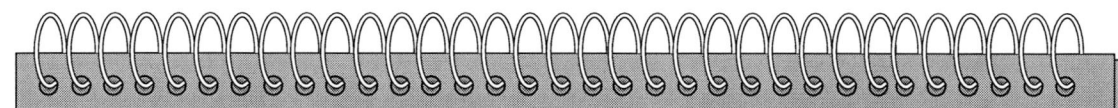

1. Who is the intended audience of this text?

2. How do you know? Write down all the features that show this.

3. What is the purpose of this text?

4. How do you know? Write down all the features that show this.

5. What persuasive techniques have been used?

6. How formal is the language? Is it suitable for purpose and audience?

7. What connectives have been used? How do they guide the reader through the leaflet?

8. What other technique has been used to structure the piece and guide the reader through?

9. The reader is often addressed directly. Why is this, and what impact does it have?

10. How does the layout of the leaflet support the purpose and help the reader to find the required information?

Darkside by Tom Becker		Lesson 14
Class:	Date:	Period:

Lesson coverage:	Chapters 25–27. Students will: storyboard a key scene; explore suspense; prepare for assessment.
As a result of this lesson:	**All students will be able to**: explain why they find a scene exciting. **Most students will be able to**: provide evidence and detail. **Some students will be able to**: consider the views of others.

Assessment focuses **Reading** **AF4**: identify and comment on the structure and organisation of texts, including grammatical and presentational features at text level. **AF6**: identify and comment on writers' purposes and viewpoints, and the overall effect of the text on the reader.	Framework objectives **3.2 Speaking and Listening**: taking roles in group discussion. **6.2 Reading**: analysing how writers' use of linguistic, grammatical and literary features shapes and influences meaning.

Resources:	• Resources 14.1 (Emotion graph), 14.2 (Storyboard)

Personal teaching notes:

Darkside by Tom Becker — Lesson 14

Class:	Date:	Period:
Starter	Ask students to complete Resource 14.1 for a character of their choice for the final three chapters. **Extension**: Use different colours to put in multiple characters.	
Introduction	The ending of the book is dramatic and exciting. Ask students to work in groups to pick the three most exciting scenes. Take ideas and reasons from them, and highlight that people may respond differently to events and characters. This is fine, as long as they provide reasons and evidence.	
Development	Using Resource 14.2, ask students to storyboard their choice of the most exciting scene.	
Plenary	Ask the question: How has Tom Becker made this story exciting and dramatic? Lead a discussion, using the storyboards as a springboard. This is going to be the focus of students' assessment piece.	
Homework	Ask students to look at their AFs and their personal targets to ensure they meet them in next lesson's assessment piece.	

14.1 Emotion graph

Darkside

Complete this emotion graph for a character of your choice from Chapters 25–27 of *Darkside*. You will need to note the key events in the chapters along the horizontal axis.

Rising emotions →

Key events →

Darkside

14.2 Storyboard

Create a storyboard of the scene you think is the most exciting in the final part of *Darkside*.

Shot number	Visuals (sketch what will be seen)	Camera, lighting, sound notes	Dialogue	Director's notes
1				
2				
3				
4				
5				
6				

Darkside by Tom Becker		Lesson 15
Class:	Date:	Period:
Lesson coverage:	Final assessment of reading and writing.	
As a result of this lesson:	**All students will be able to**: demonstrate they have improved their writing level. **Most students will be able to**: explain how they have achieved this. **Some students will be able to**: identify the next area of focus.	
Assessment focuses **Reading** and **Writing**: all AFs	**Framework objectives** Students are being assessed rather than taught to meet objectives.	
Resources	• Assessment Guidelines grids	
Personal teaching notes:		

Darkside by Tom Becker		Lesson 15
Class:	**Date:**	**Period:**
Starter	Individuals to look back at their working Assessment Guidelines grids to remind themselves of the areas they have set as focus.	
Introduction	Distribute the title for the assessment piece and quickly take ideas that might be included. Remind students of the need for their writing to be in paragraphs (using the PEAI rule will help) with clear 'flags' for the reader to follow (in the form of connectives).	
Development	Students to write assessment piece: **How has Tom Becker made this story exciting and dramatic?**	
Plenary	Individuals self assess their work against the Assessment Guidelines – grids Class discussion – what have they learned about reading and writing during this Scheme of work?	
Homework	There is obviously going to be another adventure in Darkside for Jonathan. Ask students to write the first part of this (either a paragraph or a chapter depending on ability).	

Assessment Guidelines – Reading

	AF2	AF3	AF4	AF5	AF6
L4	• I can find some points in the text which help me answer questions. • I can sometimes find quotations which help me prove what I think. • I use quotations to comment on what the writer is saying.	• I can usually work out what a character in a story is like by looking at what they do or say in different parts of the story. • I can usually work out the writer's opinion even when it is not clearly stated. • Sometimes I can say exactly which part of the text helped me work it out.	• I can identify how the writer has organised the points in a text or the events in a story. • I can sometimes comment on why the writer has decided to do this.	• I can identify some of the choices the writer has made in the language they have used. • I can usually think of a reason why the writer has made those choices.	• I can identify what the writer thinks about an incident, character or idea. • I can usually explain how I worked out the writer's viewpoint. • I can usually say what effect the writer's viewpoint has on the reader.
L5	• I can usually find all the points which will help me answer questions. Sometimes I find these points in different parts of the text. • I can usually find quotations which prove what I think. • I sometimes use quotations to comment on some of the choices the writer has made.	• I can read between the lines to comment on a character in a story or the writer's opinion, even when it is not clearly stated. • I can usually explain my deductions using evidence from different parts of the text.	• I can identify the main events in a story and the ways in which the characters change. • I can identify the key ideas in a text and the order in which the writer has put them. • I can usually explain why the writer has made these decisions.	• I can identify a range of different language features which the writer has chosen to use. • I can explain why the writer has made these choices. • I can sometimes comment on the effect of the writer's language choice on the reader.	• I can identify what the writer thinks about an incident, character or idea and what they want the reader to think about it. • I can usually find some evidence to show what the writer has done to get their viewpoint across to the reader. • I can usually explain how the writer has influenced the reader's viewpoint.

Darkside

Assessment Guidelines – Reading

	AF2	AF3	AF4	AF5	AF6
L6	• I can find all the points which help me answer questions. I often do this by collecting information from different parts of the text, or from two or more texts. • I always choose quotations carefully to prove exactly what I think. • I always use quotations to comment on the choices the writer has made.	• I can analyse a text or part of a text and work out the different meanings which the writer is implying. • I always use evidence to explain my deductions. • I usually try to comment on the writer's meanings and how I worked them out.	• I can identify how events and characters develop and change in a story. • I can identify how a writer has sequenced their points or ideas in a text. • I can comment on the effect the writer wants to have on the reader and how their choice of structure and organisation helps achieve this.	• I can recognise and name a range of different language features. • I can explain and comment in detail on the effect the writer's language choice has created. • Sometimes I can see a pattern in the writer's choice of language in a text and comment on why the writer has chosen to do this.	• I can work out what the writer thinks about an incident, character or idea based on close analysis of the writer's choice of language. • I can clearly explain the effect on the reader and comment on how the writer has created it.
L7	• I always choose my points carefully, making sure they help me answer questions accurately. Sometimes I concentrate on a particular word – and sometimes I look at a few paragraphs to work out what the writer thinks. • I always use quotations to comment on the choices the writer has made. • I always choose quotations carefully to prove exactly what I think – and sometimes I refer to other texts to support or prove my point.	• I can analyse a text or part of text and work out the different layers of meaning which the writer is implying. • I choose evidence carefully to explain my deductions. • I always try to comment on the writer's meaning by considering different possible interpretations and weighing up evidence from different parts of the text.	• I can comment on the effect the writer's choice of structure and organisation is intended to have on the reader. • I can comment on how effectively the writer has used structure and organisation to achieve this effect.	• I can comment precisely and in detail on language which the writer has chosen for effect. • I can recognise and comment on how the language a writer has chosen contributes to the overall effect of the text on the reader.	• I can comment precisely and in detail on how the writer has used language and other features to influence the reader's response. • I sometimes comment on a range of evidence from different parts of a text explaining how it shows the effect the writer wants to create and the reader's response to it. • I am beginning to realise how writer's choose certain techniques in their writing because of the effect they can have on the reader.

© Pearson Education Ltd, 2008

Assessment Guidelines – Writing

	AF1	AF2	AF3	AF4
	Writing imaginative, interesting and thoughtful texts	Producing texts which are appropriate to task, reader and purpose	Organising and presenting whole texts effectively…	Constructing paragraphs and using cohesion within and between paragraphs
L3	• I try to choose good points and ideas to put in my writing. • I sometimes use adjectives to add detail to my ideas. • I usually know what I want to say in my writing but sometimes my ideas change once I've started.	• I try to stick to the purpose for which I am writing. • Sometimes I find it difficult to use the right structure in my writing. • I try to make my writing suit its purpose.	• I try to organise the information, ideas or events in my writing by putting them in order. • Sometimes I find it difficult to decide on the best order for my ideas. • I try to make sure my opening and ending suit what I am writing.	• Sometimes I organise my sentences into paragraphs. • Sometimes I link the ideas in my sentences, but I don't use connectives very often. • Sometimes it is difficult for readers to follow the ideas in my writing because I do not always link them.
L4	• I usually choose relevant ideas or points in my writing. • Sometimes I write in detail about my ideas using adverbs and adjectives. • I don't usually change my ideas or point of view once I've started writing.	• I usually remember and stick to the purpose for which I am writing. • I usually choose the right structure to suit the purpose of my writing. • I usually choose the way I write to suit the purpose of my writing. Sometimes I forget what effect I want to have on the reader.	• I usually organise the information, ideas or events in my writing. I usually make sure my opening and ending suit what I am writing. • I usually structure my writing by putting things in the order in which they happened. • Sometimes I forget to link my paragraphs or use connectives to help the reader follow my ideas.	• I usually decide on the order in which I will put the sentences in my paragraphs. • I use some connectives to link the sentences in my paragraphs – but I often use the same connectives, eg also, first, next, then. • I sometimes link my paragraphs and use connectives to help the reader follow my ideas.

Assessment Guidelines – Writing

	AF1	AF2	AF3	AF4
L5	• I choose relevant ideas or points in my writing and sometimes I add my own ideas. • I choose my ideas and the way I write about them to suit the type of writing I am doing. • I usually stick to the point when I am writing. Sometimes my ideas change when I think about them as I am writing.	• I always remember and stick to the purpose for which I am writing. • I always choose the right structure to suit the purpose of my writing and sometimes adapt it to suit a particular task. • I always choose the way I write to suit the purpose of my writing and to keep the reader interested.	• I organise the information, ideas or events in my writing clearly. I carefully decide how I will organise my sentences into paragraphs. • I usually plan the whole piece of writing before I begin, thinking about how my ideas relate or connect to each other. • I usually link my paragraphs using connectives to help the reader follow my ideas.	• I decide the best way to put my information or ideas into paragraphs. • I use different ways to link my sentences together in a paragraph. Sometimes I use connectives, sometimes pronouns and sometimes I refer back to previous ideas. • I try to write each paragraph so that it fits into the finished piece of writing.
L6	• I always use my own ideas in my writing, choosing them to suit the kind of writing I am doing and the audience I am writing for. • I always stick to the point in my writing. I can usually match the way I write to suit what I am writing about or to suit the different voices in a story. • I usually use the right level of formality for the purpose and audience I have chosen for my writing. Sometimes I decide to vary the level of formality in a piece of writing to have a particular effect on the reader.		• I always organise the information, ideas or events in my writing, thinking about the effect I want to have on the reader. • I help the reader follow my ideas in a variety of ways: I use connectives, clear opening sentences in paragraphs, and links between paragraphs.	• I always organise and write paragraphs so that they help my writing achieve what I want to say and how I want to say it. • I carefully choose connectives (and other links between sentences) both to connect my ideas and for the effect on the reader I want to achieve.
L7	• I am confident that I can write for a wide range of purposes and audiences, choosing my ideas and the way I write to suit them. • I always know what kind of 'voice' I want to achieve in my writing, and I usually achieve it. • I always choose my level of formality and the way I write because of the effect I hope it will have on the reader.		• I always organise the information, ideas or events very carefully in my writing to suit its purpose and to achieve a specific effect on the reader. • I try to control the reader's response by deciding the order in which I will reveal events, or release information, to them.	• I decide on the effect I want my writing to achieve then plan the structure of each paragraph to suit it. • I can use a range of techniques, such as varying the length of, or sentence types in, a paragraph, to achieve different effects.

Assessment Guidelines – Writing

	AF5	AF6	AF7	AF8
	Varying sentences for clarity, purpose and effect	Writing with technical accuracy of syntax and punctuation…	Selecting appropriate and effective vocabulary	Using correct spelling
L3	• I usually write in simple sentences. • I often use connectives like *and, but, so*. • I sometimes use different tenses but not always consistently.	• I sometimes use full stops, capital letters, question and exclamation marks accurately to show where my sentences start and finish. • Sometimes I use commas to join sentences when I should use full stops to separate them. • I can use speech marks but sometimes I forget.	• I try to choose words which will help me explain my ideas but I sometimes find it difficult to think of them. • Sometimes I choose words because of the effect they will have on the reader.	• I can usually spell: – some of the words which I often see, eg *you, because, although* • I sometimes find it difficult to spell: – words where the endings have changed, eg plurals (*-es, -ies*), change of tense (*-ied, -ing*) • I usually guess more difficult words, spelling them how they sound.
L4	• I try to use a range of different lengths and types of sentences in my writing. • I use a range of connectives in complex sentences, such as *if, when, because,* etc. • I can use a range of different tenses, usually correctly and consistently.	• I always use full stops, questions marks and exclamation marks accurately. • I use speech marks accurately. Sometimes I use other punctuation inside the speech marks but I am not always sure when it is correct. • I use commas in lists. I sometimes use commas in complex sentences but I am not always sure when they are correct.	• I sometimes choose words which I think will be effective. • I sometimes spend time thinking about or looking for the best word to suit the meaning or purpose I want to achieve.	• I can usually spell: – words which I often see, eg *you, because, although* – most adverbs which end in *ly* • I sometimes find it difficult to spell: – words which sound the same as other words (homophones) eg *they're/their/there; to/too/two* – words where the endings have changed, eg plurals (*-es, -ies*), change of tense (*-ied, -ing*). • I sometimes guess more difficult words, spelling them how they sound.

Assessment Guidelines – Writing

	AF5	AF6	AF7	AF8
L5	• I use a range of different lengths and types of sentences in my writing. I use longer sentences to give more information, and shorter sentences for emphasis. • The range of connectives I use to link ideas in and between sentences is growing, eg *although, on the other hand, meanwhile, etc.* • I sometimes decide on the order in which I will write the words in a sentence to emphasise a detail or an idea.	• I use full stops, questions marks exclamation marks, and speech punctuation accurately. • Readers usually find it easy to understand my sentences because of the word order and punctuation I choose. I am often unsure where to put commas in longer, more complicated sentences.	• I always choose words which I think will be effective. • I try to use a wide range of vocabulary in my writing. Sometimes I use words when I am not entirely sure of their precise meaning.	• I can always spell: – words which I often see, eg *you, because, although* – words where the endings have changed, eg plurals (*-es, -ies*), change of tense (*-ied, -ing*) – most words with suffixes, eg *-able/-ible; -ion/-ian* – most words with prefixes, eg *dis-, un-, ex-* • I sometimes find it difficult to spell: – words with prefixes which double consonants, eg *irregular, unnecessary* • Occasionally I guess more difficult words, spelling them how they sound.
L6	• I can use a range of different lengths and types of sentence to achieve different effects, depending on the purpose of my writing. • I often select the word order and structure of a sentence to achieve a particular effect.	• Readers always find it easy to understand my sentences because of the word order I choose and the accuracy of my punctuation. I am occasionally unsure where to put commas in longer, more complicated sentences.	• I always choose words which I think will be effective for the purpose and audience of my writing. • I try to use the full breadth of my vocabulary although sometimes I use the wrong word because I am not sure of its precise meaning.	• I usually spell most words correctly. • Occasionally I spell more difficult or unusual words incorrectly.
L7	• I often use a particular type or length of sentence to achieve a specific effect or contribute to the overall purpose of a text. • I can select the word order and structure of a sentence to convey my meaning and purpose with some precision.		• I always choose words which I know will be effective for the purpose and audience of my writing. • I aim to use a wide and ambitious range of vocabulary which I select carefully for precision of meaning and effect.	• I spell most words correctly, including more difficult or unusual words.